Bear Grylls

SURVIVAL SKILLS HANDBOOK

SHELTER BUILDING

Bear Grylls

This survival skills handbook was specially created to help young adventurers just like you to stay safe in the wild. Spending the night in the wild can be a great experience, and a good shelter can mean the difference between life and death. This book will show you the best places to build a shelter, how to build a shelter with materials you've found in the wild, and, most importantly, how to stay alive in the most extreme conditions.

Bear

CONTENTS

WHY WE NEED SHELTER

Food, water, and shelter are the three most basic things needed to stay alive. A good shelter will help to protect you from harm, and can make you feel better in a difficult situation. It can give a sense of security and belonging, as well as keeping you warm, dry, and safe from predators.

Factors to consider

Before building a shelter, it is important to consider its purpose.

Size

How many people need to get into the shelter? Do you need space to store equipment? Small shelters are usually quicker and easier to build, but may not be fit for purpose if there are a lot of you, or if you are planning to use it for more than a night or two.

What do you need protecting from?

Consider what dangers are present in the environment around you. Are there wild animals in the area? What are the weather conditions like? This will determine how sturdy the shelter will need to be, and what materials you should use.

How long can you spend building it?

It's usually much easier – and safer – to build your shelter during the day, when there is plenty of light and fewer predators. How many hours of daylight do you have left?

How long will it be needed?

An hour? A night? A week? This will determine whether you need a simple shelter to protect you from a short downpour, or a sturdier shelter that will last for a long time.

Location

Is it in a good place? Do you want to be hidden or easily found? If you are staying in the shelter for longer than a day, you will need access to food and water. Is the shelter near a source of water?

BEAR SAYS

It's a good idea to practise building a shelter before you go on an adventure. Try building one in your garden or local park using natural materials.

USEFUL TOOLS AND MATERIALS

A variety of tools and materials can be used to build a shelter. If you know you will be building a shelter before you start a trip, you should take some or all of this equipment with you. If you are caught short, you will need to work with what you have with you, or can find in the wild.

Tools

If you are planning to build a shelter in the wild, it is a good idea to take these vital tools with you. Be very careful, as sharp tools in careless hands can be very dangerous. If possible, ask an adult to use them for you.

axe

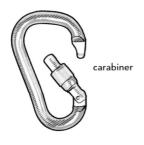

carabiner

saw

knife

torch

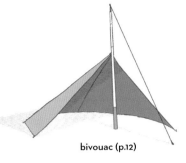

bivouac (p.12)

Camping equipment

Taking some or all of this equipment with you when you spend a night in the wild will make your time much more comfortable and enjoyable.

gloves

fuel

tarpaulin

ice pack

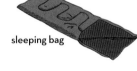

sleeping bag

lighter fluid

lighter

tongs for charcoal

sleeping mat

gas or battery powered lantern

portable picnic table

cooking utensils

food cooler

charcoal or kindling

barbecue

More useful tools and materials

Shelters can be built from any number of different materials – from specialist equipment, to items you may have with you, and materials you can find in the wild.

Rope
You can buy strong, lightweight rope from camping shops, but in a push you could use string, or even parachute cord.

Wooden poles
If you don't have tent poles with you, look for straight, thick sticks or branches instead.

Parachute
These are incredibly handy, particularly in wet climates. They can be used to keep rain off you, your equipment, and your campfire.

Shovel
Shovels can be used to dig fire pits, sleeping trenches, and even toilets!

Army poncho
This lightweight item is one of the most useful pieces of kit you can bring. You can wear it over your clothes and bag to keep dry, and it can be quickly turned into a waterproof shelter with very little other equipment (p18).

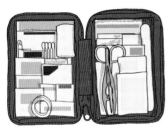

First aid kit
You should always bring a first aid kit with you on any adventure, even a short hike.

Mobile phone
Assuming you have signal, a mobile phone (and portable power bank) can be a life saver if you need to call for help.

Sleeping bag
Nowadays, sleeping bags are very lightweight and easy to carry.

Hammock
It is often safer to sleep off the ground, particularly in wet conditions, or if there are dangerous animals like snakes or scorpions around.

BEAR SAYS
If you want to start a fire, make sure you do it at a safe distance from your shelter and keep a bucket of water, sand, or earth nearby to avoid flames spreading.

Matches
Keep your matches in a waterproof bag – they will be no use if they get wet!

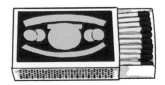

TENTS

If you know you will need shelter and can carry it, the most sensible option is to bring a tent with you, or arrange to use one that is already at your destination.

Campsites

It's worth checking to see if there is a campsite in the area you are planning to spend the night. These are usually quite cheap to use, and will save you carrying heavy camping equipment with you.

Carrying your own tent

In the old days, tents included a heavy piece of tarpaulin and several large, wooden poles. Nowadays, you can get lightweight tents that will fit easily in your rucksack.

Cycling

If you are planning an adventure where you will be cycling, you can use a special bike trailer to transport your camping equipment. You may find this easier, as you won't need to carry a heavy rucksack.

BEAR SAYS

If you've never been camping before, go with someone who can show you what to do, and enjoy it – it's really good fun!

Bivvy bag (bivouac)

Sometimes a bivvy bag can be a good option. A bivvy bag is essentially just a waterproof bag that is big enough for you, your sleeping bag, and sleeping mat. They are extremely small and light to carry, but the protection they give is minimal.

Bivvy shelter

A bivvy shelter has a little bit more structure than a bivvy bag, but not as much as a tent. It is still a very snug fit, but is an excellent emergency option, and can make a huge difference in cold or wet conditions. Bivvy shelters are very light and pack up very small.

BEAR SAYS

Remember that a layer underneath is worth two on top – natural insulation to lie on is critical to conserve heat.

Things to consider when choosing a tent

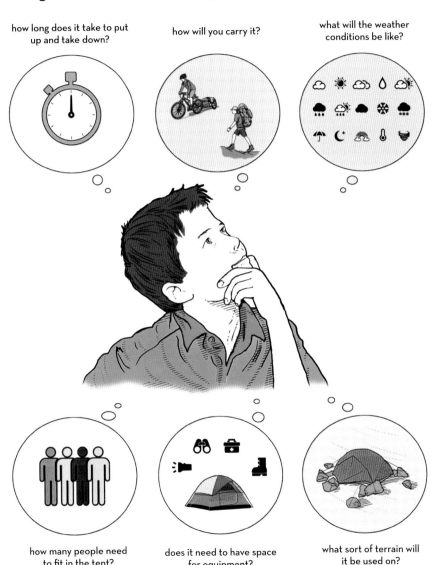

how long does it take to put up and take down?

how will you carry it?

what will the weather conditions be like?

how many people need to fit in the tent?

does it need to have space for equipment?

what sort of terrain will it be used on?

CHOOSING A PLACE TO BUILD A SHELTER

The ideal location of a shelter is often not properly thought out. People can be very keen to gather materials before checking the area is safe and convenient. Making a rushed decision ultimately means that your shelter might need to be moved or rebuilt. Take time to look around the available area, and remember that conditions can change. The situation will be different depending upon whether you are in a survival situation or just camping out for the night.

Water
Place your shelter near to water, but not so close that you risk getting swept away.

Predators
Make sure you choose a location that is safe from predators and poisonous or prickly plants.

Make use of natural features
of the landscape as much
as possible – you might save
valuable time and energy.

Wind direction

If you are in a hot climate, you might want the
prevailing wind to come into the mounth of the
shelter. If not, it is best to position the shelter to
protect you from the wind.

Natural shelters

Sheltering in a cave or
cluster of trees can save
you time and energy, but only
if it is safe to do so.

Resources

You don't want to carry
anything further than
needed, so build your shelter
close to building materials.

Trees

Large trees can provide good shelter, but be carefu — a hanging dead branch is called a "widow maker" fo a reason. Sleeping on a roc can also be uncomfortable so check the area before y set up camp.

widow maker

Fire

Keep fire in a safe place where it won't get out of control. Avoid building a fire under trees, as you could set fire to the roots or overhanging branches.

Rocks

Large rocks, or boulders, work well as a natural windbreak.

Animal pathways

Keep an eye out for animal pathways.
Lots of animals are nocturnal. You may
find yourself sleeping in the equivalent
of the forest's motorway if you're not
careful.

BEAR SAYS

The location of your shelter can
mean the difference between
life and death, so take time to
think about it.

Ditches

A gully or a ditch should be avoided –
it may turn into a river if it rains.

BASIC SHELTERS

There are almost endless ways to build a shelter. The best shelters are adapted to suit the conditions, but here are some ideas to start you off. It's worth experimenting and practising shelter building when you aren't in an emergency situation.

practise shelter building at home

Poncho shelters

A poncho is a very useful piece of survival equipment. It is basically a large waterproof sheet with a hole in the middle and an attached hood. You can wear it, wrap things in it, or make it into a shelter. It is useful if you choose a good quality material to avoid leaks and tears. Grommeted corners (with a hole in them) are also helpful when attaching it to your structure.

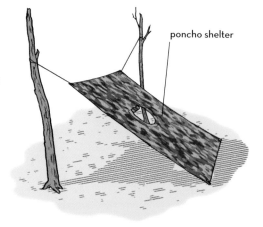

poncho shelter

Basic lean-to shelter

1. Choose a location.
2. Stretch the poncho out to measure the area of ground to clear.
3. Move the poncho away and clear the area of debris.
4. Attach a strong string or rope between two vertical posts or trees about 60 cm off the ground (this will depend on the size of the person).
5. Attach one of the longer sides of the poncho to the rope – tie with string using the grommets to help.
6. Attach the other long side of the poncho to the ground. Secure using a tent peg or stake through the grommets, keeping it taught and closing the hood if necessary.

BEAR SAYS

If you are using your poncho to build a shelter, you will probably need to tie the hood to close the hole up.

attach a strong string between two vertical posts or trees

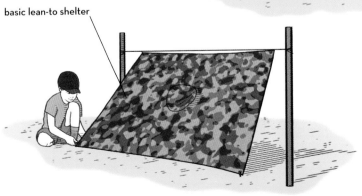

basic lean-to shelter

One-person shelter

1. Tie one end of a long pole to a tree around waist height.
2. Lay two heavy, slightly shorter poles on the ground, facing the same direction as the first pole.
3. Hang a sheet over the top pole so there is the same amount of fabric hanging over each side.
4. Tuck the sides of the sheet under the bottom poles and lay any spare material inside the shelter to act as a floor.
5. You can place an extra pole at the entrance to stop the poles moving inwards, or hammer some stakes into the ground.
6. If you have spare material, use it to make a door at the entrance.

Emergency blankets

These blankets are also known as space, survival, or Mylar blankets. They are very lightweight and often silver coloured. They may be useful for a smaller person, or for building a shelter for firewood or equipment, but they are a bit small to shelter an adult. They are also very easily damaged by windy conditions.

Making an emergency blanket shelter

An emergency blanket won't be big enough to build a one-person shelter, but could be used to build a shelter similar to a poncho shelter (p18). To prevent the fragile material from tearing, wrap the corners around small pebbles and tie them with cord.

BEAR SAYS

Knowing how to make even the most basic of shelters could save your life in an emergency.

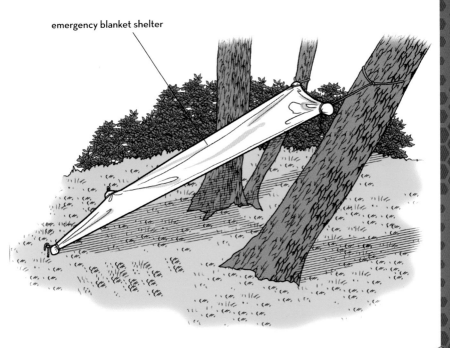

emergency blanket shelter

Debris hut

This shelter is warm, fast, and easy to build if suitable materials can be found. It's a simple design, and can be built large enough for two people.

1. Tie a long, sturdy pole on top of a tree stump or other suitable base at around waist height.
2. Place several large sticks along both sides of this pole, creating a wedge shape. Make sure the shelter is big enough for you to fit inside, and that the sides are steep enough so that rain will run off.
3. Put thinner sticks or other materials between the large sticks, making a sort of mesh to stop anything falling into the sleeping area.
4. Add plenty of grass or leaves over the mesh until the sides are at least one metre thick – the thicker the better.
5. Put some heavy branches on top of the grass or leaves to stop it blowing away.
6. Get a pile of leaves or grass ready so that you can pull it over the entrance as you get inside.

make a wedge shape using large, sturdy sticks or poles

create a "mesh" using smaller sticks

BEAR SAYS

If you can, add some leaves or grass to the inside of the shelter to act as insulation. This doesn't need to be as deep, and will help to keep you warm.

cover the shelter with leaves and grass

Debris lean-to shelter
This can be built with virtually no tools or equipment.

1. Find or make two uprights about 2 m apart. Trees would be ideal.
2. Tie a horizontal pole or branch between the two uprights at chest height.
3. Lean 6–8 branches or poles (around 3 m long) against the horizontal pole at around a 45° angle, and push them into the ground. Make sure the shelter is facing the right direction so the wind blows onto the back of the shelter.
4. Use thinner, bendy branches to weave a lattice through these poles.
5. Cover the lattice with leaves or any other fine material you can find, starting at the bottom and piling it up.

45°

HOT CLIMATES

In a hot climate it is vital to have a shelter that will protect you from the many dangers these climates present. Your shelter must protect from sun, heat, wind, rain, and any dangerous animals, such as snakes or scorpions.

Beach shelter
You will need: something to dig with, driftwood to use as supports.

1. Look for the high tide mark (usually the highest point where debris has been washed up). Build above this line so your shelter won't get washed away.
2. Dig a trench that is big enough to lie in. Face it North-South so it receives the least amount of sunlight.
3. Pile up the sand to make sides.
4. Lay driftwood across the sides and top to create a roof and stop the sand collapsing inward.

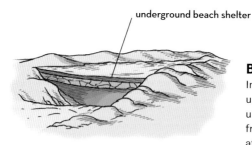

underground beach shelter

Below ground desert shelter
In some situations, sheltering underground may make sense. An underground shelter can protect you from heat, as well as cold, animal attacks, and extreme weather. However this shelter will take more effort to build than one above ground. If it is very hot, it might need to be done at night when it is colder.

creating a double cover will help to keep the temperature down if you have enough material

Jungle A frame shelter

This is a more complicated shelter that will need practise to perfect. A knowledge of knots would be useful in order to secure everything tightly. This shelter will keep you off the ground, away from insects and snakes.

1. Take two long, sturdy sticks, connecting them at the top to create an A shape. Secure this with a smaller stick tied about halfway down. You will need two of these.
2. Find three long poles of a similar length. Secure each end of one to the top of your A frames, then rest the other two on the connecting poles to create a hammock area.
3. Tie the structure securely with rope or string (if you don't have rope, parachute cord or vines will do).
4. Secure one poncho or tarp as a roof, and the other as a hammock. The hammock will need to be firmly tied, taped, or even sewn, so it can safely hold a person.

jungle A frame shelter

BEAR SAYS

If you can learn about different knots, you will find that you have less trouble getting your shelter to work every time.

COLD CLIMATES

In cold climates, a good shelter can mean the difference between life and death. A cold-weather shelter will need to protect from wind, rain, snow, and cold.

Tree pit snow shelter

This will work if you are near to evergreen trees and lots of snow. A shovel or something to dig with would also be helpful.

Dig down around the trunk of the tree as far as you need, and pack the snow tightly to make the sides and the entrance firm. Use branches to sit on, and to cover the top of the hole.

BEAR SAYS

Make sure you mark the outside of your shelter with something brightly coloured to make it easier to find.

Snow cave

1. Choose an area with deep snow if possible.
2. Pile up snow to make a mound, packing the snow firmly as you go.
3. If possible, leave the snow for a couple of hours so it can harden – your shelter will be firmer this way.
4. Dig a tunnel into the mound and hollow out the inside of the cave. Smooth the inside to prevent drips.
5. Make ventilation holes and carve benches to sleep on.
6. Keep your shovels inside the cave with you, so you can dig your way out in case of an avalanche or blizzard.

WET CLIMATES

The most difficult shelters to build are ones to keep you dry. Heat and cold are much easier obstacles to overcome. If you know you are going to be out in the rain, it is always worth packing a poncho or a waterproof sheet so that you can keep the rain off. Being wet is extremely miserable, especially when you are trying to sleep.

swamp bed

Swamp bed

1. Find four trees, or drive posts into the ground to make strong uprights. Make sure there is room for you and your equipment.
2. Two long poles need to be lashed to the uprights. Make sure they are high enough to keep you dry, allowing for the maximum amount the water will rise.
3. Tie shorter poles across to form the platform.
4. Cover the top of the platform with leaves, grass, or any other soft material to make a more comfortable sleeping surface.

BEAR SAYS

If you don't have a waterproof sheet, bracken or turfs could be used as roofing material if the structure underneath is strong enough to support it.

Bracken foundation

This is built when the ground is marshy or too wet to sleep on. It's basically a thick mattress of sticks and twigs that spreads you weight over a large area to prevent you sinking. The twigs are laid in layers, and each layer is laid at right angles to the last one. The uprights are then driven through the mattress to support a cover.

BEAR SAYS

This isn't a shelter – it's a raised platform that would keep you dry and off the ground in wet or muddy conditions.

bracken foundation

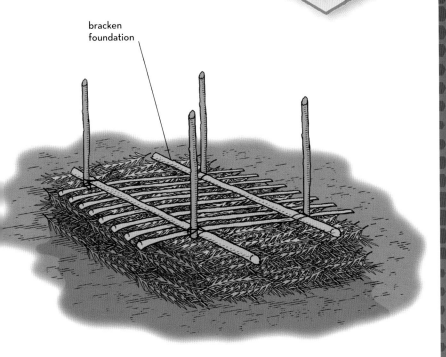

SHELTERING IN TREES

If you can, it is often a good idea to shelter in trees rather than on the ground. This will put you out of the reach of most predators and other dangerous animals, especially if you are in the rainforest or somewhere else with a lot of wildlife.

Parachute hammock

1. Cut out a piece that contains six segments (slices) of a parachute.
2. Fold one segment over the next and then again, so you have a sleeping surface made up of three thicknesses of fabric.
3. Find three trees that are a suitable distance apart, and tie the base of the parachute between them using parachute cord.
4. Tie an awning line higher up in the trees, and drape the remaining segments over it. Tuck in the final segment, and add stabiliser bars.

parachute hammock

BEAR SAYS

If you have suitable trees in your garden or local park, it is a good idea to practise building hammocks before you go adventuring.

Tree boat hammock

This is a piece of camping equipment that can be bought to make life simpler. It isn't particularly light, but if you know you want to sleep off the ground, and you want a hammock that doesn't tip or shut around you, then this option is definitely worth considering.

tree boat hammock

TEPEE TENTS

These simple tents are constructed from a parachute, some cord, and poles, and can range in size depending on the materials available.

You will need:

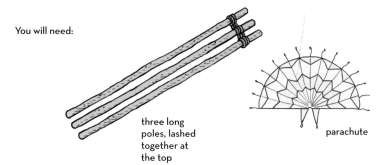

three long poles, lashed together at the top

parachute

1. Stand the three poles together in a tripod position.

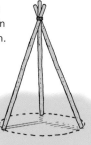

2. If necessary, add extra poles to ensure your tepe is sturdy.

3. Drape the parachute evenly around the poles, fastening securely at the top.

4. If you intend to have a fire in the tepee, leav an open space at the top for ventilation.

Building a tepee tent

This can be tricky at first, and it's a good idea to practise building a tepee tent beforehand if possible. One of the best things about tepee tents is that you can do a lot of your preparation in advance, cutting your poles and tying them together, so the shelter can be assembled relatively quickly and easily once you reach your destination.

Tree tepee

If you don't have any suitable poles, it is possible to make a tepee tent by gathering the material of your parachute together at the top and lashing it to a tree branch. Use tent pegs or stakes to fasten the parachute to the ground to give the tent its structure.

BEAR SAYS

If possible, use a piece of tarpaulin or a second parachute to create a groundsheet for your tepee tent to help keep you dry.

pole-free tepee tent

BUILDING A FIRE REFLECTOR

This simple reflector can be made from wood, rocks, or soil – basically any material that is easy to get hold of. It doesn't have to be fancy – it just needs to be a flattish surface built behind a fire.

Benefits

- Reflects light and heat into your shelter.
- Directs smoke upwards and away from you.
- Acts as a windbreak.

wooden fire reflector

How to build a fire reflector with soil and wood

1. Find a spot about 30 cm from the fire, and about 80 cm tall and 60 cm wider than the fire.
2. Sharpen three medium-sized stakes and drive them into the ground.
3. Place larger logs between the stakes to the correct height – you may need to tie the stakes or the logs together.
4. Fill any gaps with soil.
5. You can build more than one fire reflector if needed.

SURVIVAL STORIES

Building a shelter can be fun, but it is also a very important survival skill. Many explorers have saved their own lives by building a shelter to protect them from adverse conditions.

Scott and Haston

In 1975, Doug Scott and Dougal Haston became the first explorers to climb the southwest face of Mount Everest. After reaching the summit, they made the highest snow shelter that had ever been constructed at that time. By midnight, there was no oxygen left in their breathing apparatus and their stove had run out of fuel. The temperature was estimated to have reached -50°C. They would have died if they went to sleep. Instead, they kept moving and massaging each other to keep warm.

Doug Scott as a young climber

Doug Scott

Returning to camp

They made it down to the nearest camp after 30 hours without food or sleep and, surprisingly, neither of them suffered frostbite. It had taken them 33 days in total to ascend, which was the fastest climb of the mountain at that time.

BEAR SAYS

Scott and Haston's story is an amazing example of survival. Explorers train for years to be able to survive in Everest's extreme conditions.

Mount Everest

Columbian survival

A man from Cambridge was carrying out a Colombian weasel conservation project in the cloud forests of Colombia in 1994. He got lost, and eventually realised he wasn't going to find his way back before dark. He made a bivvy bag by wrapping a poncho around himself, and put his feet in a rucksack to stay dry overnight. He decided to sleep on a ridge to avoid landslips that regularly occur in the area.

Colombian weasel

He made a raft of sticks to raise himself off the damp ground and away from biting ants.

biting ants

He was aware that there were pumas in the area, so he collected bioluminescent fungi to provide light, and kept his machete next to him for protection. The next morning, he followed a stream down a ravine, but fell down a waterfall and was knocked out. Luckily, he wasn't too badly hurt and managed to carry on walking and eventually found a road and was taken to safety. Fresh puma footprints were seen in the area.

bioluminescent
fungi

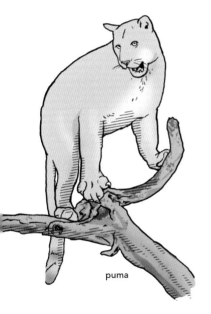

puma

puma footprint

SLEEPING COMFORTABLY AND STAYING WARM

Building a shelter to keep yourself dry is important, but it's also very important to keep yourself as warm and comfortable as possible, as it often gets much colder at night, even in the desert. If possible, you should bring warm clothes and a sleeping bag with you on any adventure where you are planning on spending one or more nights in the wild.

Tents and sleeping equipment

While shelter building is a very useful skill, the most practical shelter in the wild is a tent. If you know you are going to be spending the night in the wild, it is a good idea to take a tent with you. A sleeping bag will keep you warm, and an inflatable mattress will keep you off the cold ground, as well as being much more comfortable.

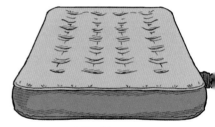

inflatable mattress

sleeping bag

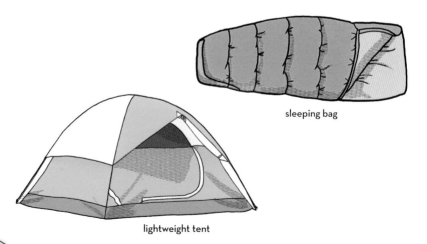

lightweight tent

Natural sleeping surfaces

If you do not have an inflatable mattress or sleeping mat, heather or bracken can make your sleeping area softer. Make sure to clear the area of debris first – sleeping on stones or uneven ground can be very uncomfortable.

clear the area

heather can be used to make a natural mattress

Campfires

It often gets much colder at night, so a campfire is invaluable when it comes to keeping warm. If it is particularly cold, you can sleep next to the fire to stay warm. Campfires can also keep away dangerous animals and insects, cook food, and provide a sense of comfort and security in a tough situation.

SLEEPING WITHOUT ANY SHELTER

There may be occasions where you cannot find any materials to build a shelter, and need to spend the night outside.

Survival tips

- If you can find a forest or wood, then the trees can provide shelter even if you can't reach any shelter building materials or haven't got any tools.
- Try and choose a location away from any animals that might disturb you. Insects can be a real problem if you choose to sleep close to their routes.
- Use the natural environment to help you – sleeping under a hedge or next to a rock might offer some protection.
- Scrape a dip in the ground if you can.
- Choose the driest place possible.
- Check above in case anything could fall on you in the night.

BEAR SAYS

Sleeping outside should be an absolute last resort – always try to build or find shelter if possible.

look for natural windbreaks

- Make sure you know about any dangerous wildlife in the area. Sometimes the safest option if you are approached by an animal is to do nothing, while other situations may be dealt with by running, fighting, shouting, or climbing trees.
- Be careful about what you eat and drink. Educate yourself about what is helpful and what is harmful.
- A ditch might be a good location, giving some protection from wind, but be careful it isn't going to turn into a river if it rains.
- If you are with somebody else, huddle together to share body heat.
- You will feel very exposed – it may be worth deciding if it is safe for you to carry on travelling rather than stop.

be aware of dangerous wildlife

never eat wild mushrooms unless an adult with plant identification training tells you it is safe to do so

be wary of ditches

SAFETY

The single most important thing on any adventure is safety – both yours and that of everybody you are with. Before you go on a trip, make sure you have the right equipment and are prepared for any problems to ensure that everyone is safe.

Burns

1. Keep yourself safe – you can't help anybody by putting yourself in danger.
2. Stop the burning by removing the person from the area, putting water on the flames, or smothering flames with a blanket.
3. Remove any clothing or jewellery that is close to the burnt area, but don't try and take off anything that is stuck to the skin.
4. Run the burn under lukewarm or cool water. Never use ice or any greasy substances.
5. Keep the person warm.
6. Cover the burn with cling film or a clear plastic bag.
7. Get an adult to provide a suitable painkiller medicine.
8. Sit them upright if the face or eyes are burnt.
9. Get them checked by a medical professional, even for a minor burn.

put out the flames using a blanket, jacket, or damp towel

pour lukewarm water on the burn

cover the burn in clingfilm

Cuts

Press on the area with a clean, dry, and absorbent material for a few minutes. If something is stuck in the cut, leave it there until you can get medical advice. You might need to press on either side of it. Elevating the arm or leg helps reduce the flow of blood. When the bleeding has stopped, wash and dry the cut and put a dressing on.

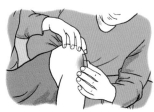

put pressure on a cut

Bruises

Hold an ice pack on the bruise as soon as you can, for up to ten minutes. A bag of frozen peas in a tea towel will do the job if you don't have an ice pack. If you don't have anything frozen, use a clean, damp cloth. If the bruise is extremely swollen, painful, or doesn't go away on its own, or if it was caused by a bump to the head, medical advice is needed.

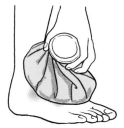

hold an ice pack on
the affected area

Splinters

Make sure you have clean hands.

For a small splinter, clean the wound with water. If it doesn't hurt, the splinter will work its own way out if it is left alone. If it hurts, you can gently touch the area with sticky tape and see if that pulls it out.

If the splinter is larger, clean some tweezers with alcohol. If you can see the end of the splinter, grip it with the tweezers and pull it out in a straight line. Squeeze the wound to make it bleed slightly, as this will help remove dirt. Wash and dry the wound and pop a dressing on if needed.

always make sure you
have clean hands when
handling injuries

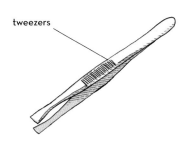

tweezers

BEAR SAYS

Never put yourself or anyone else at risk. If you must, postpone a trip if you think the situation is going to be too dangerous.

GLOSSARY

Absorbent – something that soaks up liquid easily.

Bioluminescent – a living organism that gives out light.

Conservation – the protection of animals, plants, and natural resources.

Debris – loose natural material or rubbish.

Embedded – an object that is fixed firmly in its surroundings.

Frostbite – an injury to body tissue caused by extreme cold.

Fungi – single-celled organisms that produce spores, e.g. mushrooms, mould, or mildew.

Grommet – an eyelet placed in a hole to reinforce it.

Gully – a ditch or channel cut by running water.

Insulate – to keep something warm.

Obstacle – something blocking the way.

Predator – an animal that stays alive by killing and eating other animals.

Prevailing wind – the most frequent wind direction experienced at a particular location.

Ravine – a deep, narrow gully with steep sides.

Segment – a portion.

Splinter – a small, thin sharp piece of material that has broken off a larger piece.

Tarpaulin – a heavy duty waterproof cloth.

Tweezers – small, metal nippers or pincers.

Discover more amazing books in the Bear Grylls series:

Perfect for young adventurers, the
Survival Skills series accompanies an
exciting range of colouring and activity
books. Curious kids can also learn
tips and tricks for almost any extreme
situation in *Survival Camp*, and explore
Earth in *Extreme Planet*.

Conceived by Weldon Owen in partnership
with Bear Grylls Ventures

Produced by Weldon Owen Ltd
Suite 3.08 The Plaza, 535 King's Road,
London SW10 0SZ, UK

WELDON OWEN LTD
Publisher Donna Gregory
Designer Shahid Mahmood
Editorial Susie Rae, Claire Philip, Lydia Halliday
Contributor Anne Farthing
Illustrator Bernard Chau

Disclaimer
Weldon Owen and Bear Grylls take pride in doing our best to get the facts right in putting together
the information in this book, but occasionally something slips past our beady eyes. Therefore we
make no warranties about the accuracy or completeness of the information in the book and to the
maximum extent permitted, we disclaim all liability. Wherever possible, we will endeavour to correct
any errors of fact at reprint.

Kids – if you want to try any of the activities in this book, please ask your parents first! Parents – all
outdoor activities carry some degree of risk and we recommend that anyone participating in these
activities be aware of the risks involved and seek professional instruction and guidance. None of the
health/medical information in this book is intended as a substitute for professional medical advice;
always seek the advice of a qualified practitioner.

A WELDON OWEN PRODUCTION. AN IMPRINT OF KINGS ROAD PUBLISHING.
PART OF THE BONNIER PUBLISHING GROUP.